EAT LIKE A LOCAL- SYRACUSE

Syracuse New York Food Guide

Kenya Sumter

Eat Like a Local-Syracuse Copyright © 2020 by CZYK Publishing LLC. All Rights Reserved.

All rights reserved. No part of this book may be reproduced in any form or by any electronic or mechanical means including information storage and retrieval systems, without permission in writing from the author. The only exception is by a reviewer, who may quote short excerpts in a review.

The statements in this book are of the authors and may not be the views of CZYK Publishing.

Cover designed by: Lisa Rusczyk Ed. D.

CZYK Publishing Since 2011.

Eat Like a Local

Lock Haven, PA
All rights reserved.
ISBN: 9798697705117

BOOK DESCRIPTION

Are you excited about planning your next trip? Do you want an edible experience? Would you like some culinary guidance from a local? If you answered yes to any of these questions, then this Eat Like a Local book is for you. Eat Like a Local - Syracuse by author Kenya Sumter name offers the inside scoop on food in Syracuse New York. Culinary tourism is an important aspect of any travel experience. Food has the ability to tell you a story of a destination, its landscapes, and culture on a single plate. Most food guides tell you how to eat like a tourist. Although there is nothing wrong with that, as part of the Eat Like a Local series, this book will give you a food guide from someone who has lived at your next culinary destination.

In these pages, you will discover advice on having a unique edible experience. This book will not tell you exact addresses or hours but instead will give you excitement and knowledge of food and drinks from a local that you may not find in other travel food guides.

Eat like a local. Slow down, stay in one place, and get to know the food, people, and culture. By the time you finish this book, you will be eager and prepared to travel to your next culinary destination.

OUR STORY

Traveling has always been a passion of the creator of the Eat Like a Local book series. During Lisa's travels in Malta, instead of tasting what the city offered, she ate at a large fast-food chain. However, she realized that her traveling experience would have been more fulfilling if she had experienced the best of local cuisines. Most would agree that food is one of the most important aspects of a culture. Through her travels, Lisa learned how much locals had to share with tourists, especially about food. Lisa created the Eat Like a Local book series to help connect people with locals which she discovered is a topic that locals are very passionate about sharing. So please join me and: Eat, drink, and explore like a local.

TABLE OF CONTENTS

BOOK DESCRIPTION
OUR STORY
TABLE OF CONTENTS
DEDICATION
ABOUT THE AUTHOR
HOW TO USE THIS BOOK
FROM THE PUBLISHER
1. Your Destiny Awaits
2. Tully's, A Syracuse Classic
3. Say Uncle Chubby's
4. Weekday Brunch, Weekend Dinner
5. Seafood Fit For a King
6. Fine and Brine
7. Think Bigg, Eat Big
8. Go and Seek Heid's
9. DMV Sushi
10. Barbequed Dinosaur
11. Limping Lizard
12. Go To Peppino
13. Strolling To Avicolli's
14. No Pain, No Grain
15. Dream Pita
16. Get Funky
17. Strong Hearts For A Strong Stomach

18. Otro Alto
19. Mello Velo
20. Thai Love NY and NY Love Thai
21. Apizza Regionale in Syracuse
22. Bleu Monkey Blues
23. Mission Accomplished
24. Glazed, Dazed, and Amazed
25. Stout and Shout
26. Ancient Greek Treats
27. Lemon Grass Pass
28. Francesca's Cusine
29. A Dose of Grill
30. Phoebe's Fee
31. Goodie Grill
32. Stuck In The Middle
33. The Landmark
34. Yes Fair
35. Orange Lake
36. Almost Ivy League
37. Be There at Armory Square
38. Hot Hops
39. Unlimited Pastabilities
40. Puts The York in New York
41. Hoynes Joyness
42. Melt At the Modern Malt
43. Blue Tusk Is a Must

44. Evergreen and Evermore
45. Can Ya Get Sakana-Ya
46. Try Nick's Tomato Pie
47. Eating at Eden
48. A China Cafe You Say
49. Wine and Whiskey That's Not Too Risky
50. Cookin In the Cookie Kitchen
BONUS TIP 1 The Mall
BONUS TIP 2 Armory Square
BONUS TIP 3 Taste of Syracuse
Resources:
READ OTHER BOOKS BY CZYK PUBLISHING

DEDICATION

This book is dedicated to everyone in my home city of Syracuse who helped me be where I am today. Thank you to my family, teachers, friends, and anyone else who believed in me.

ABOUT THE AUTHOR

Kenya Sumter is a student who resides in Syracuse. Kenya loves to write, read, make music, and appreciate art. Due to living in Syracuse her whole life, she knows tons about the food in Syracuse and what the city has to offer. She is currently a student and one day hopes to spread creativity to the world.

HOW TO USE THIS BOOK

The goal of this book is to help culinary travelers either dream or experience different edible experiences by providing opinions from a local. The author has made suggestions based on their own knowledge. Please do your own research before traveling to the area in case the suggested locations are unavailable.

Travel Advisories: As a first step in planning any trip abroad, check the Travel Advisories for your intended destination.
https://travel.state.gov/content/travel/en/traveladvisories/traveladvisories.html

FROM THE PUBLISHER

Traveling can be one of the most important parts of a person's life. The anticipation and memories that you have are some of the best. As a publisher of the *Eat Like a Local*, Greater Than a Tourist, as well as the popular *50 Things to Know* book series, we strive to help you learn about new places, spark your imagination, and inspire you. Wherever you are and whatever you do I wish you safe, fun, and inspiring travel.

Lisa Rusczyk Ed. D.
CZYK Publishing

Eat Like a Local

Don't Skip Syracuse

"To eat is a necessity, but to eat intelligently is an art."

-François de la Rochefoucauld

Syracuse is a small city known for two things; snow and college basketball. Although those are the most famous things about it, there are many hidden treasures beyond that. Even the residents of the city may not know of all of the cultural foods waiting to be unearthed. Syracuse has a large volume of people from different cultures bringing in their own food. This place is ideal for those who like the environment of a city, but can't afford big city prices, those who like the cities and the suburbs, and those who would like to drive from where they are to where they need to be in about 15 minutes. There are hot summers and rough winters which gives this city character a sense of spontaneousness throughout the year. Furthermore, there is a diverse range of people who live in the city coming from all over the world proving this city is something special. So without further ado, here are my 50 suggestions of places to eat in Syracuse.

Syracuse
New York, USA

Eat Like a Local

Syracuse New York Climate

	High	Low
January	32	15
February	34	17
March	43	25
April	57	36
May	69	47
June	77	56
July	82	61
August	80	73
September	73	52
October	60	42
November	48	33
December	37	22

GreaterThanaTourist.com

Temperatures are in Fahrenheit degrees.
Source: NOAA

Eat Like a Local

1. YOUR DESTINY AWAITS

I simply can't mention Syracuse without bringing up THE Destiny USA. What makes this mega mall so special is that it is the main attraction of Syracuse drawing people from all over New York and even Canada as it's the largest shopping mall in New York and the 6th largest in America. Also being the 48th largest mall in the world, this 6 story center has grown in size since 1990, previously going under the name, the Carousel Mall due to the big carousel ride one can ride on in the food court. The food court has a ton of restaurants to dine giving people Popeyes, Starbucks, Koto Japanese Steakhouse, Charleys Philly Steaks, and Cajun Cafe & Grill to name a few. But those are just some of the places. Ever since the mall expanded to its mega-size status, it expanded itself to restaurants like the Cheesecake Factory, Johnny Rockets, 110 Grill, Cantina Laredo, and Dave and Busters. There are almost too many things to do since there are 239 stores to shop from major big brand centers to local stores and tiny set up shops that come and go. There are also two movie theatres, the top 2 floors used for events like fashion shows, proms, or other private occasions, and a wide array of entertainment like Apex entertainment arcade, the

Funny Bone stand up comedy stage, glow in the dark golf, laser tag, and more things that'll be built in the future. If you come to Syracuse and don't come to the mall, you're missing out on a huge part, but there is another smaller part you should stop by as well.

2. TULLY'S, A SYRACUSE CLASSIC

You'll have a good time here, according to the slogan promises. This family-owned restaurant has been operating since 1991 and has expanded to other locations across New York and even Pennsylvania serving food perfect for you and whoever you want to dine with. To get started, there are appetizers you can practically smell through the menu since they got nachos, fries, wings, dip, quesadilla, and other bar-like food. For another offer you can't refuse, there's tenders, homemade soup, and salad entrees. If you want dinner or lunch, which I know you do since that's why you're here, have yourself some deli sandwiches, favorites from Tully's including fish tacos, meatloaf, and smothered chicken, sandwich platters, burgers, pasta, meats, and healthy options with vegetarian foods. Just in case sodas and water aren't strong enough for you, you can enjoy drinks anytime or during happy hours on the weekdays from 3 pm-7 pm or late night from Sundays thru Thursdays from 9 pm to closing time. Drinks offered are draft specials, wine, spirits, vodka, shandies, sangria, Gatorade drinks, hard teas, margarita, and enough alcohol of other varieties to fill up a room. These desserts are a nice treat to top off your night serving you peanut butter chocolate cookie monster cookies, chocolate peanut butter pie, chocolate chip cookie monster, and pumpkin cheesecake. The only thing this place is missing is pizza, but there is a restaurant to satisfy your saucy needs.

3. SAY UNCLE CHUBBY'S

Offering authentic New York (and yes, New York, New York) style food upstate, Uncle Chubby's says that you will never have to cook again. From sheet pizza, New York Style Pizza with toppings like nacho cheese, taco meat, meatballs, jalapenos, pepperoni, sausage, mushrooms, and ham. You can also take a dive into their specialty pizzas as they got Mexican pizza, Philly cheesesteak, meat lovers, chicken wings, super breakfast, kitchen sink, veggie pizzas. And that's just their pizzas. They offer seafood, hot subs, sandwiches, salads, burgers, pasta, and fish for your dining pleasure. In addition to all those options, fries of all kinds (including nacho and loaded), hot dogs, garlic bread, nachos, mozzarella stick, and pizza logs are only some of the available sides, and sweets like deep-fried Oreos, cookies, cheesecake, brownies, and Doggles (cinnamon fried dough) can finish you off. You can see how Uncle Chubby's has that name and nobody can blame you if you gain a pound or two. If you like filling food then there's even more for you to eat in this town.

Eat Like a Local

4. WEEKDAY BRUNCH, WEEKEND DINNER

Do you like big meals with a vintage flair and be surrounded by Betty Boop while eating. If yes, then that is a really specific fantasy, but it is a reality in the form of a diner fit for you. Stella's Diner has a couple of locations in Syracuse New York to serve your appetite and if it's big, then you're in luck. The spontaneous menu has serving sizes that match the big prices attached to each dish which includes omelets, toast, eggs, pancakes, breakfast sandwiches, and cereal with sides of grits, oatmeal, sausage, apple slices, and then some. Dinner selections are burgers and fries, sandwiches, wraps, salad, and seafood. Even though the food may be a little pricey for a diner, it's worth every bite since half of one meal can be enough to fill you up. Not only will you have dinner for a couple of days, but their weekly specials will show as a surprise to those who like to try new things. If dinner isn't filling you up, their desserts will make your cake, pudding, shakes, floats, and ice cream sundaes for your appetite. If you want to eat there, go get them while it's hot because from Sundays to Thursdays it's open from 6 am-2:30 pm and on Fridays and Saturdays they're open from 6 am to 8 pm. What if you want more seafood? Well, there is a restaurant that is fit for a king and it's in Syracuse as well.

5. SEAFOOD FIT FOR A KING

If you're looking for a seafood restaurant without the busy ambiance of most seafood restaurants then this may be for you. Located in Mattydale, King Seafood is a quaint little restaurant that will give a feel at home vibe to your luxurious dinner. This establishment also offers unique choices too such as mozzarella sticks, boiled eggs, chicken wings, orange juice, sandwiches, and sausages. Your servings of seafood can even come in full sizes so you can feel like you're getting your money's worth but hopefully, you'll have room for dessert. The mouth-watering desserts displayed on their website will leave you wanting to make room for more. So if you're ever looking for the sea in the middle of Mattydale, then you're in luck for some fine food. But what if it's too expensive for you? Don't worry, there is another restaurant with smaller prices for your wallet's sake.

6. FINE AND BRINE

The Brine Well Eatery is not as high scaled but has big meals for small prices. Named after cities in New York, These filling plates come with at least two sides and some sauce to top it all off. On top of that, if you don't like the custom meals, you can customize your own plates with no additional charge and get 2 entree choices with it. This place even offers a Caesar salad as a vegan option, fried cheese curds, fried pickles, and baked beans as sides. The website of the restaurant even has an interactive chat system so any of your questions about it can be answered within minutes. Not a ton of hot and spicy food is offered, but fortunately, there is another place that provides it.

7. THINK BIGG, EAT BIG

Mr. Biggs is called that for two reasons; big food and big smiles. If you're looking for jerk food from a friendly environment then Mr. Biggs is the place to go. Since 2013, it's been their mission to serve the finest Jamaican food around and that is a mission they seem to accomplish. From oxtail, signature Mr. Bigs rice, curry chicken, plantains, and jerk chicken, these full portions can fill you up and still leave you wanting more. The hot food is perfect to combat the unrelenting cold climate of Syracuse bringing authentic food and quick services. Although it is understandable if this jerk food is too hot to handle, but there is something cooler to put in your mouth.

Eat Like a Local

8. GO AND SEEK HEID'S

One of the oldest restaurants around Syracuse, Heids in Liverpool is a hot dog restaurant, their deal is Hofmann dogs making them stand out from other restaurants. If the name Heidi's sounds familiar to you, then you probably heard it on the show, 'Man vs. Food' which gained attention due to its popularity, drawing in customers from all over the country. Their menu consists of Hofmann franks, double franks, mixed doubles, a double snappy, Gianelli sausage, Philly cheesesteak, grilled cheese, and chicken tenders. For sides, there is so much to choose from such as chips, macaroni salads, onion rings, fries, chili, and fried pickles. They serve standard sodas with their drinks and shakes, but if you want a special treat then, there are brownies, cookies, and puff corn. This place is perfect for a relaxing lazy summer day, but what about when you have a business to take care of? Well, there is a restaurant for that too.

9. DMV SUSHI

If you ever craved a meal while at the DMV then Yamasho Sushi Steakhouse has got you covered. Although not open on Mondays, this Japanese steakhouse offers meats, seafood, and poultry blended together with the special sauce that sets this restaurant apart. The appetizers are enough to sell you on a trip, the meals come with its signature soup, salad, 2 piece shrimp, vegetables, and the choice of steam fried rice, fried rice, or noodles. That's right, all of those things come with the main dish as either a dinner entree or a combo. From 3:30 to 6:00 happy hour runs with a special menu that consists of rolls, salads, and tunas along with a wide selection of alcoholic beverages including wine, sake, and cocktails. For the youngins eating out, their menu is half the size of the adult menu, soft drinks with free refills for some, and ice cream. Let me show you another famous restaurant in Syracuse that you cannot miss out on. Introducing…

Eat Like a Local

10. BARBEQUED DINOSAUR

This is the first Dinosaur BBQ to open up and the rest are imitators. Expanding to New York City and Newark, New Jersey this is the OG Dinosaur BBQ that opened in early 1920 seating up to 125 people in the establishment and on the balcony. Don't let all the tattoos and bikers scare you away, their food is superior and worth the so-called risk. Their starters are fried green tomatoes, bbq chicken wings, bbq chili nachos, and creole deviled eggs. The dinners are worth every cent and every minute you wait since they serve you the hottest food including chicken, ribs, bbq wings, salads, specialty bowls, pulled pork sandwiches, burgers, brisket sandwiches, and chicken steak. They have two kinds of sides; hot ones which are bbq beans, fries, mac and cheese, chili, simmered greens, and mashed potatoes then there are the cold sides which are coleslaw, cottage cheese, side salad, macaroni salad, and tomato-cucumber salad. The only thing keeping me from this place daily is the prices, but there is another place that is close enough.

11. LIMPING LIZARD

I know you're not made out of money, so if you're craving Dinosaur BBQ, but don't have Dinosaur BBQ money, then go for the smaller animal known as Limp Lizard. Serving a similar ambiance and live music while you're eating at this bar and grill has three locations for those who want it. When the weather is decent, they also have an outdoor BBQ to draw you in and to show you all that it has to offer. Limp Lizard offers appetizers known as Tastebud Teasers pretzels, nachos, buffalo fries, and pigskin. Their appetizers may be enough to put them ahead of the game, but their main entrees such as their ribs, wraps, sandwiches, tender, and customizable burgers will determine that for good. Mix that with their tex-mex meals and side dishes, it makes more sense as to why this restaurant has two locations within a 15-minute drive. Syracuse is known for its Italian food so now, let's take a look at some of them.

Eat Like a Local

12. GO TO PEPPINO

Syracuse, appropriately named after the city in Sicily, has a sizable Italian population in the city which gives it one of the best Italian restaurants. They serve pizza, subs, calzones, breakfast foods, and deep-fried Oreos which goes above and beyond regular Italian restaurants. Peppino's is an award-winning restaurant that has been operating for over 50 years and has reinvented itself by adapting to the times. They've partnered with the Oncenter War Memorial Arena which is a venue that hosts events like graduations, concerts, and conventions and has a food truck that will show up to your house or event you're hosting. That's right, the restaurant will pull up to wherever you're staying at and let you choose a part of their menu for three hours accompanied by two personal chefs. For all of that, it's safe to say they deserve the awards and high customer ratings they received. Somewhere a few miles away, there is another popular Italian eatery as well.

13. STROLLING TO AVICOLLI'S

This modest Italian restaurant in Liverpool has been called the best at take out food in the area and it's all made from scratch. Since 1984, they've been serving dishes like New York-style pizza, paninis, sandwiches, pasta al Forno, and so much more Italian goodness. If you want a little something before you get into dinner, they have appetizers like subs, salads, pasta al Forno, mozzarella sticks, greens, and more. Even at a little place like this, there is beer, wine, and cocktails to choose from with non-alcoholic drinks being offered too. If you also ever wanted Italian desserts as well, then you're in luck here since they serve treats like tiramisu, gelato, chocolate cannoli, and housemade lemon ricotta cake. All of that and more deserve any acclaim that this restaurant can get. What about vegetarian and vegan options as some may say? Well, have no worries because there are tons to choose from here.

14. NO PAIN, NO GRAIN

Original Grains is a vegetarian-friendly restaurant with a hip vibe and an easy to navigate interface on the site. Its signatures include thinking outside of the box and inside of a bowl as they have many from smoothie bowls, grain bowls, green bowls, and noodle bowls. The main grain that this place is known for is pita which comes in their tacos and gyros. To drink, they have matcha, mocha jefe, coffee, tea, beer, wine, cider, and a selection of smoothies. For their sandwiches, they come on French bread with gluten-free or multigrain options. As the typical millennial restaurant that Original Grain is, they offer toasts with some gluten-free options, and yes, of course, they have smashed avocado toast. So many people seem to like Original Grain so much, that they can get gift cards worth up to $50 for next time. Now how about we go somewhere a little more Mediteranianer?

15. DREAM PITA

Pita Dreams has all of the Mediterranean halal food you could desire with a convenient delivery service. That's right, delivered to your home by Grubhub, Doordash, or Ubereats could be a piece of the Mediterranean waiting to swim in your mouth. They have platters that come with yellow rice, pita bread, and garlic sauce like the beef kafta, gyro, loaded dream fries, and falafel. There's also pitas of course that come in the same forms as the platters and both come with sides. Sides include original fries, garlic fries, signature dream fries, hummus with pita, falafel, and baklava. All of that with a choice of hot, dream, garlic, or tahini sauce sounds like a dream itself but there is more to it. They even have a food truck that you may be lucky enough to catch on the prowl in the streets of Syracuse so there is still a way for you to come to them. If you need some breakfast in your life then there's a diner that's nice and funky.

Eat Like a Local

16. GET FUNKY

Funk 'n Waffles gives its customers fun flavored waffles and funky live music staying true to their slogan get down and eat up. For breakfast, you can get a waffle breakfast, omelet scramble, fruit, and egg sandwiches that come with the side choices of sausage, eggs, bacon, chicken waffle fries, and home fries. There are too many varieties of waffles, and thinking about it makes my head spin, but I'll tell you the best items you can chow down on. You can have chicken and waffles, waffles with strawberry and whipped cream, waffles smothered in chocolate, waffles smothered in gravy, vegan waffles, ice cream on waffles, and waffles you can customize with any kind of bread, batter, and toppings they have. Available, there is also chicken 'n fries, grilled sandwiches, and disco fries and you can have waffle shipped to your house or even take individual ingredients home-like pure maple, tofu, muffins, ham, gravy, banana slices, and Nutella with the addition of getting clothing merchandise, hat pins, stickers, drink chips, and gift cards as items. All the food sounds deliciously unhealthy, but what about a delicious and healthy restaurant? We got you covered.

17. STRONG HEARTS FOR A STRONG STOMACH

Looking for the most vegan restaurant in Syracuse? Strong Hearts on the Hill is possibly the most vegan-friendly restaurant in the city serving up casual dining since 2008. Offering nachos, salads and sandwiches, it appeals to those who eat meat and encourages them to consider going vegan with healthy options. To clench your thirst, they also offer milkshakes named after significant historical figures from the Martin Luther King, Jr. mocha to the Nat Turner chocolate banana milkshake. Top that meal off with their selection of desserts which consists of Recess Chocolate Chip Cookies and a rotating selection of cupcakes that have allergy-friendly options for those who can't consume nuts, soy, and gluten. If you still want a little something after your meal, you can cop a shirt to show off your love of the restaurant. All of the foods here are cold, but rest assured there are places that serve spicy Mexican food.

Eat Like a Local

18. OTRO ALTO

Otro and Alto Cinco are two different restaurants owned by the same person just to clear that up (For a year I thought they were the same place and was super confused) The former was built in 2013, 19 years after Alto Cinco which serves more refined food than it's little sister restaurant which consists of salads, tacos, enchiladas, pizzas, burritos, nachos, tostadas, quesadillas, with sides of yellow rice, beans, chicken, steamed spinach, fried catfish, grilled shrimp, bbq tofu, and jalapenos and all of those things can be topped off with sauces like red sauce, guacamole, sour cream, mayo, and ketchup. There's also juice, soda, and wines to drink and cookies and vegan brownies for dessert. As for Otro Cinco, they have whatever Alto Cinco doesn't have like shrimp, catfish, tofu, calamari, paellas, tazones, burritos, quesadillas, and soup. If you can't choose between which of the two you want, another is always waiting for you to enter.

19. MELLO VELO

In a city that does a good job catering to its college population, Mello Yello is a restaurant that can repair your bike while you eat. As hipster as it sounds, you can rent, buy, or get a bike repaired at this cafe and get a bite to eat. Being the hipster restaurant that it is, they obviously have vegan and vegetarian options, serving breakfast (which is all day by the way), lunch, and dinner. The items on their list are clearly indicated to be vegan or gluten-free such as pesto tofu scramble, vegan rancheros, and falafel burger, and options for non-vegans like pancakes, tonkatsu pork sandwich, and chicken gyro. To drink with it, you can get beer, wine, cocktails, and more for alcohol, and for non-alcoholic drinks, you can choose drinks such as coffee, smoothies, milk, lemonade, or soda. To top this place off, Mello Yello has a bakery with sweet-smelling goods like brownies, scones, pies, and more that you can enjoy in the cafe or on their outdoor deck. As great as all these restaurants sound, what about the fancy and classy eateries? Don't worry, Syracuse has got you covered.

Eat Like a Local

20. THAI LOVE NY AND NY LOVE THAI

If you're craving a little bit of Los Angeles in Syracuse, then the closest you can is some Thai food. Thai Love NY and that restaurant name stays true to the statement since their food fills your stomach and heart. One can almost smell the food off the menu. It's almost impossible to not want to taste it. Shrimp, rolls, wings, and omelets are just a few of their appetizers and just one look of their soup makes you want to drink every drop from the bowl. If you ever wanted to try curry then you're in luck as they have seven flavors of it which are red, green, yellow, pineapple, panang, massaman, and jungle curry. Thai Love NY includes fried rice, omelets, and noodles which can be accompanied by sauteed meat complemented by other ingredients to make the flavor pop. Along with the seemingly never-ending list of noodles and rice, a kids meal serves things that the kid would want or try like dinosaur nuggets and fried tofu. Even the desserts have rice in it which may seem eyebrow-raising, but when you get just a whiff of the raspberry sticky rice or coconana, those raised eyebrows will be raised out of happiness. If you want somewhere a little more downscale and less pricey, I know a place.

21. APIZZA REGIONALE IN SYRACUSE

Yes, this place is an Italian restaurant in Syracuse (there are tons). Apizza Regionale blends the tastes of Italian cooking with the hometown feel that they put in their food. Serving the typical Italian dishes, they offer antipasti which is a slight alternative to regular pasta like grass-fed meatballs, zucchini fritte, and olives and cheese. Although the budino dessert sticks out as a chocolate hazelnut pudding with almond brittle, the bar really sets this restaurant apart. Most tend to forget that a defining part of Italy is the wine and other drinks and this restaurant doesn't neglect to highlight it. From the reds, the whites, the rose, sparkling, Birra, cocktails, and gems by the bottle, they come and go based on what you like. Not only will you have an international taste, but the menu also shows where the alcohol is from and what year it was made. Just drink responsibility, they'll show how big the glasses you can get and what's in the cocktails. If you want something a little more casual, then the next place will make you feel like you're at home.

22. BLEU MONKEY BLUES

Bleu Monkey Cafe located near the college campus, Bleu Monkey Cafe is a casual looking and feeling Japanese cafe. This sushi restaurant adds a modern flair that appeals to the local students with their reasonable prices and diverse options. For their appetizers, they have seafood mixed with their unique dressing some of which can be a meal in itself. Not only do they offer soups and salads, but they have special boxes that are served with rice, a side salad, a spring roll, and 4 pieces of California roll. Mix that with a choice of noodle bowls, over rice dishes, curry, nigiri, and sashimi and rolls, it leaves many options for anyone who wants to eat. You can even try Japanese soda or tea as a drink if you want something unconventional. Ice cream and cheesecake can be the last thing you put in your mouth to finish the whole experience. Of course, if you want to go somewhere more popular, then there is a place for you to enjoy.

23. MISSION ACCOMPLISHED

The Mission Restaurant exists to give its customers Mexican and Latin food and a vibrant atmosphere. This is also one of the most highly acclaimed restaurants in Syracuse as it has positive reviews from customers, food critics, and even the Huffington Post, this restaurant has been able to wow people no matter who they are or where they're from. The Mission is also a historical landmark since this used to be a stop in the Underground Railroad and a church. Now, they're known for appetizing dishes such as Mexican fries, taquitos, and queso fundido. After that, you can choose from salads with either shrimp, steak, or shrimp, chicken tortilla or black bean soups, burritos, tacos, enchiladas, quesadillas, stew, fajitas, and special wraps which are wrapped in cheddar jalapeno flour tortilla with fries. You can't have a meal like this without a good drink and The Mission gives you milk, Goya juices, sparkling water, tea, lemonade, sodas, bottled Saranac, and (saving the best for last), cocktails produced with wine-based spirits. If only this establishment served glazed desserts. I think you know where this is going.

Eat Like a Local

24. GLAZED, DAZED, AND AMAZED

A restaurant with the name Glazed and Confused can't be a restaurant that takes themselves too seriously and they don't. The colorful and cartoonish restaurant was founded just four years ago in 2016 as just a small shop. The menu serves up mouthwatering and literal cartoonish donuts from The Springfield which is a strawberry glaze with (or without) sprinkles, the confused cinnamon and sugar, and the blackout chocolate cake donut and the confused dozen so if you can't choose, you can get 1 donut of each flavor of your choosing with vegan and gluten-free options on Wednesdays and Saturdays. Those are just the classics, but for the confusing options, you can be served a cinnamon roll donut, the pardon my french toast which is a maple glaze with cream cheese frosting and vanilla streusel, and the cereal killer which is vanilla cake dipped in honey glaze topped with cereal. All of those donut options and more are there for eating pleasure and they even serve up their signature doninis defined by them as a delicacy pressed like a panini and served on a classic cake donut. Serving drinks like milk, iced tea, soda, and coffee, before you leave, Glazed and Confused also has a store in which you can buy any other products that you can keep or donations to any fundraisers they're affiliated with. Now that's what I call a restaurant with a sweet spot, and I bet this next place will fill your other sweet spot.

25. STOUT AND SHOUT

Stout Brewing Company is a Brewery near Westcott with many beers to drown your worries in. Open from 5 pm-10 pm on the weekdays and from 2 pm-10 pm on Saturdays, this place offers draft and pitcher beers and ales of your choice. Their regular rotation consists of Phil Irish Stout, Maurice Triple Chocolate Stout, Ben Black Wheat, and more. As for their seasonal rotation, you can be treated to Mason Tart Cherry Stout, June Strawberry Rhubarb Ale, and Cooder Caramel Apple Porter. If you want something to snack on with it, you can treat yourself to a big soft mighty pretzel, sammiches of either roast beef or seitan meats, subs, pickles, or personal pizzas. Why don't we go back to the sweet stuff with the next choice?

Eat Like a Local

26. ANCIENT GREEK TREATS

Hercules Candies is one of the oldest bakeries in Syracuse founded in 1905 under different names. Whether it was called the Boston Candy Kitchen, The Hercules Candy Company, or Hercules Candy, this generational family business was founded by a Greek immigrant family who honed the skills of candy making. All of your sweet desires can come to fruition here as they have anything you may need for any occasion. Chocolate candy bars, ribbon candy, and even vegan candy. They have a combination of chocolate candies displayed on their website from chocolate marshmallows, backward chocolate chip cookies, coconut clusters, and peanut butter milk chocolate covered potato chips. For special occasions, this place has got you covered as they have assorted chocolates for anniversaries, weddings, birthdays, holidays, and if you're feeling extra nice and just want to give someone you like a special treat to eat whether it's in the form of an invitation, favor, gift bag, or little novelty treats. Even with merchandise, this place manages to go above and beyond by offering shirts, tote bags, mugs, hats, bottles, and even puzzles. No wonder why this place has stood the test of time. Enough with the sweet talk. Let's get a little more serious.

27. LEMON GRASS PASS

Established as one of the best restaurants in Central New York, LemonGrass restaurants is an award-winning bistro with an eye and stomach appealing cuisine. If you want to start off hot and spicy, their appetizers consist of fresh oysters, dumplings, steaky bacon, rolls, shrimp cocktails, and wings. Their starters of salad come in their own unique fashion and their soups consist of either Thai beef salad or the soup of the day giving a rotating selection for the ones who need a little spice in life. Speaking of spice, the entrees consist of spices of the main dishes that make them unique including their curry, steak & chops, pow, and beef. To drink, they serve up some of the finest sparkling & champagne, white & rose, red, and beers & brews around. If you're still up to the challenge, Lemon Grass Restaurants serves plated desserts such as mousse, cake, sorbet, and ice cream.

28. FRANCESCA'S CUSINE

Yet another Italian restaurant in the heart of Syracuse's Little Italy, Francesa's Cucina serves people amazing local recipes, handed down from generation to generation. Open at dinner hours, items amongst their popular foods on their menu in Italian include shrimp cocktails, seafood Utica greens, crab-stuffed shrimp, and calamari as appetizers. As main dishes, they offer up ravioli, fish, chicken, and veal amongst other meats. Like many other Italian restaurants, they serve up red and white wine by the bottle or glass in addition to the other drinks available such as chardonnay, sauvignon blanc, riesling, rose, and sparkling from Italy, California, France, and other places around the world. The next stop for restaurants on this list will be India.

29. A DOSE OF GRILL

To spice things up in Syracuse, Dosa Grill offers up Indian lunches and dinners as authentic and deliciously as possible. Having a large buffet to choose from, Dosa Grill offers appetizers including, but surely not limited to, lamb chop, chicken lollipop, Dahi poori, and achari fish fry.

Fish & shrimp, tandoori bread, soups, and salads are just a few of the main dishes you can munch on. They also serve up a wide selection of specials, such as biryanis/rice, chicken, goat, lamb, and something else made in the oven that can fill you up as well. If you don't want meat or gluten then you can choose from those menu selections such as hari bhari sabji, chickpea masala, and okra masala. If you have enough room for more, you can choose to chow down on their desserts which consist of kheer, ras malai, and fruit custard. Let me take you somewhere a little more comfortable and colorful.

30. PHOEBE'S FEE

Phoebe's Restaurant and Coffee Lounge has been a long-running bistro since 1976 with colorful rumors about the building flying around since. A favorite for theatergoers from the Syracuse Stage nearby, it's a convenient place to have lunch and dinner at. For lunch, you can munch on some small plates like fried dip, hummus, and fried zucchini, salads, sandwiches, and bistro fares. During the dinner time, one can dine on some of the same things plus entrees such as chimichurri steak, lemon garlic chicken, and veal

Milanese dishes. On Thursdays, they have the 'three-course Thursday' special with the choices of lemon garlic chicken, seared salmon, shrimp linguine, or summer vegetable risotto. To drink, there are many cocktails to taste from such as the wild berry old fashioned, peach whiskey martini, and the cool as a cucumber cocktail along with other choices of alcohol like draft beer, bottle beer, or their fine wines. For dessert, one can try the creme brulee with vanilla custard, the blueberry-pomegranate sorbet mixed with berries, or the flourless chocolate torte mixed with berries as just a couple of their options. If you need another good option, then you'll love the next place.

31. GOODIE GRILL

If you need to dive into some good tasting Mediterranean food then Goodies Mediterranean Grill & Cuisine is the place to go. Although it is not a place you can dine in, it is somewhere where you can enjoy Mediterranean food on the go or wherever you're staying. Their appetizers and Mazza consists of dolma, hummus with pita, fries, feta cheese and olives, and baba ganoush with pita. With that and more, you can choose between lentil with spinach soup or one of their salads and there are tons of drinks to go with the meal such as chocolate milk, hot tea, Turkish coffee, lemonade, juice, and soda. Their selection of entrees comes in the authentic Mediterranean form or Americanized form from much to choose from such as the fresh never-frozen burgers, sandwiches, kibbeh, kabobs, vegetarian falafels, and shawarma to name a few. If you always wanted to try Medditerranian dessert, they have baklava with walnuts, fingers, and cashews served to be chowed down on. How about we go to another part outside of the Medditaranin for the next place.

32. STUCK IN THE MIDDLE

Munjed's Middle Eastern Cafe is a family-owned bar and restaurant in Syracuse since 1984 serving up Middle Eastern and Greek dishes. Also available is an outdoor eating space and an indoor tv while you eat so you can enjoy it in whichever environment you desire. Open 7 days a week, this restaurant is also a great place for a banquet of any kind giving you access to their special catering menu. With their authentic Middle Eastern and Greek menu, they offer falafel, kabobs, different kinds of shawarma, chicken

Eat Like a Local

that comes in many different forms, gyros, spanakopita, and so many other Middle Eastern and Greek food you just have to see for yourself. Desserts include walnut baklava, cashew baklava fingers, Burma, and baklava cheesecake which claims it'll be famous soon, but that'll be left up to people. If you want some cultured entertainment then a place nearby is just right for you nearby.

33. THE LANDMARK

Opened in 1928, the Landmark Theatre offers showings of old Depression-era films, plays, and Broadway musicals that blessed the city with their musical magic. Having its highs and lows, from closing and renovating itself over the decades, it has the financial support to make sure it stands strong. This place has hosted some of the most famous acts in the world from Jerry Seinfeld, Jackson Browne, and Celtic Woman. The design of the exterior makes you feel like you're gonna see a Broadway Show, but the interior is what really captures the eye as it captures the essence of theatre by making it reminiscent of old and golden English theatres. That way if you ever decide to get married or host an event in the

Landmark Theatre you can feel like royalty, hosting an event for their subjects and associates. If you're here in the summer, there's one place you have to go to.

34. YES FAIR

For 18 days in August and September, Syracuse becomes the home of the New York State Fair and has been doing it for close to 200 years. Like most fairs, there are tons of games to play like shooting games, hoops, dart, and typical fair games along with rides and the Ferris wheel where all the other rides are. I remember as a kid, I would go into this little funhouse maze and What sets this far apart is that it brings people from around the country as it is New York's biggest yearly event bringing hundreds of thousands of people. Agriculture is a big part of Upstate New York and it is shown off in the fair, displaying thousands of animals to be displayed for the event. There are also other venues to be explored such as the Center of Progress Building, the Pan African Village, the State Fair Coliseum, the Horticulture Building, the Art and Home Center, the Youth Building, and concert stages where you can

Eat Like a Local

attend free concerts from local to world-famous artists. Food comes in multiple varieties as there are different vendors around letting you try food from different cultures or odd foods like deep-fried Oreos. Since this event takes place in the summer, it would be nice to admire nature and take a stroll. This is where the next place comes in handy.

35. ORANGE LAKE

Onondaga Lake Park is just a bit of a way away from Syracuse in Liverpool giving you the perfect view of the lake and a feel of the atmosphere. You'll be able to take your kids to one of the playgrounds and then go on a walk while viewing the city skyline. The lake is good for boating and for the row teams to compete in making the only drawback is the fact you can't swim in there, so don't go into the water. Trust me, I've been living here my whole life and the lake is no good for swimming but it's perfectly fine for admiring. There are events that take place throughout the lake like lights on the lake at the beginning of winter, antique fest, and charity runs. People sometimes have big barbecues with their family and get married around the lake too. If you're up for it, you can visit the Amphitheater concert hall or the Salt Museum. A part of the skyline you can see just about everything that makes Syracuse Syracuse, but there is one huge thing I should mention.

36. ALMOST IVY LEAGUE

Although not an Ivy League school, Syracuse University is one of the most prestigious colleges in the state and the #1 Party School in America. That's right, this school is #1 at partying and has good programs for journalism and sports literature as it is home to the Syracuse basketball team which is the thing most people are familiar with. You can attend a memorable game at the famed carrier dome, have wild escapades that might be epic enough to be reported in Syracuse's Barstool Instagram, and get a five-star education. This much fun doesn't come for free (unless you have a full-ride scholarship in which case, lucky you) tuition is at the prices of Ivy League schools at about 70k with an acceptance rate of 50%. If you do get accepted, you'll get the full college experience and join the ranks of other notable alumni such as Dick Clark, Clario, Vanessa Williams, Lou Reed, and Aaron Sorkin. Here you'll feel like royalty

Eat Like a Local

as the buildings look like castles and the city was made to serve you in a literal and figurative sense. Afterall, Armory Square was basically made to cater to the students so why not see what they have.

37. BE THERE AT ARMORY SQUARE

A small neighborhood in Downtown Syracuse, Armory Square seems to hold some of the most fruitful and colorful gems of the city. Popular amongst the local students and shoppers, one could spend all night just indulging in the art and nightlife in the district. For the day, there is the Erie Canal Museum, the Everson Art Museum, and the Museum of Science and Technology where the kids can have fun while learning about science. If you still have time in the day, you can also take a look at the Rosamond Gifford Zoo or just walk around and take in the small city atmosphere. Now, if you're looking for the nightlife, then you came to the right place. Bars and clubs rule the night with names like Benjamin's On Franklin, Trexx, and The Locker Room, to enjoy the night with others. There are still so many restaurants in the square to list off, and they reside in this district to help bring it to life as well.

38. HOT HOPS

In this so-called modern dining space, The Hops Spot serves you the feel of a casual bar with some fun on the side. Not only does this place host events for holidays and the Superbowl, but it has a game room where you and your friends for the night can play darts, bocce ball, corn hole, video games, board games, and enjoy events like stand up comedy and bingo. There's so much fun to have, you can have a private party to bring your friends together for whatever reason. You can't have a good time like this without some drinks so go ahead and get treated with some cocktails and signature long islands. If you're hungry, there are tons to choose from like their starters and snack, the poutine fries, vegan and nonvegan salads, house burgers, more amazing vegan food, and gluten-free options. Some of these dishes are hilariously named and swear to be delicious so if that and fun don't entice you, nothing will, but if you want Italian in the square there is no shortage of those.

Eat Like a Local

39. UNLIMITED PASTABILITIES

Pastabilities is an Italian restaurant different from the others in this city since it has focused on one food in particular; kale. No, just kidding, Pastabilities is an Italian restaurant open 7 days a week for lunch and dinner for 35 years. To start off strong, they have drinks like rose sangria, blackberry lemon tea, apple whiskey sugar, and mai tais to drink with your meal. Daily food specials consist of fettuccine, chili braised short rib hummus, honey lemon ranch fried chicken, and other options that rotate day to day, that just prepares you for what else is in store for you. As for pasta, there is a large array of choices that you can not only choose to customize yourself but can have made for you like pesto, linguine, cheese ravioli, carbonara, beef short rib, and cheeses smothered in whatever you desire. There's even a bakery, serving bread, focaccias, deli food, and even certain ingredients you can take home and make yourself. What makes this place so special is that it doesn't keep their recipes or foods a secret or under wraps as you can bring some of their hot sauces and noodles home to cook for yourself. If you want to taste New York then this next place will give it to you in style.

40. PUTS THE YORK IN NEW YORK

There is this one place, the York can also be found in Armory Square and is found to be a highly rated restaurant by the people it serves. Bringing his experience and flavors from the Big Apple, the York has a chic and modern vibe in the bar and lounge to set the atmosphere. The menu at the York rotates with every season, having a worldly take on the menu. Weekly specials have options of shrimp tempura rolls, chicken riggies, pulled pork sliders, pork chop, linguine and clam, prime culotte cut (sirloin), and the axe handle. For dinner there's a ton of appetizers you'll love like oysters, york nachos, bone marrow, crab rangoon, street corn, and cast iron meatball along with the york salad and caesar salad. If you really want to get into the main dishes, there's the York burger, chicken tacos, Nashville hot chicken, bolognese, the sandwich, and Faroe island salmon and you can choose the sides of either fries, crostini, kale brussels, cabbage blend, Trufe, or Parmesan Fries. The food menu might not be much, but the drinks are something else since they got all kinds of draft beer, bottles, cans of beer, beer ciders, white wine, red wine, rose, champagne and sparkling, and cocktails that'll make you forget all about it. All of that during happy hours on Wednesdays, Thursdays, and Fridays from 5 pm - 7 pm, you can also get bacon cheeseburger mac and cheese, york nachos, crab rangoon, chicken tacos, wings, or a york burger and drought beer along with flatbreads. Where's all the Irish food? We'll get to that next.

41. HOYNES JOYNESS

Okay, I think I covered almost every prominent ethnic food in Syracuse except for Irish, but if only there was an Irish pub somewhere in Armory Square. Oh wait, there is. Kitty Hoynes is an Irish bar that's old enough to drink as of 2020, serving Irish foods, and Irish drinks to enjoy. Every day, their menu features something different such as soups of the day, hot plates, sandwiches, and mussels which can be added on to their list of starters that includes brussels sprouts, Irish poutine fries, wings, and flatbread. They got salads with chicken in it too and Irish food like shepherd's pie, Irish breakfast, and Hoyne's fish and chips and for dessert, you can have their chocolate chip cheesecake, carrot cake, and blueberry upside-down cake. A bar can't be a bar without alcohol of course so I'm saving the best for last by showing you the bar menu. They got authentic Irish beers, stouts, ales, whiskey, wines, ciders, and cocktails. Let's take a look in the modern world and see another place in Armory Square.

42. MELT AT THE MODERN MALT

I know you'll probably want something more modern after seeing all of these ancient restaurants so The Modern Malt might be for you. Named as such after their refined and vintage vibes that manage to appeal to the young in a modern way. Founded only in 2014, it had the idea of bringing fun and culture together for a unique experience. Their breakfast menu is immaculate since they serve chicken scramble, vegetarian omelet, lobster benedict, and breakfast quesadillas. They even give Denny's a run for their money since they serve blueberry pancakes, bacon and banana pancakes, Tahoe pancakes with white chocolate, and oreo french toast. That's just breakfast, for lunch and dinner they have too many delicious stuff like poutinerie, sandwiches, burgers, soups, and salads with sides like eggs, bacon, sausage, ham, salads, and fries to fill you up. If you want to drink something strong they have some cocktails to go with your food like mimosas, bloody marys, and poinsettias. Not only do they have assortments of cupcakes, pies, cheesecakes, and cupcakes as desserts, but they have so many good shakes like fruity pebble shakes, German chocolate, Oreo cookie, banana fosters, and so many others. Hoping to the next bar, here is the next restaurant.

43. BLUE TUSK IS A MUST

If you want to hop into another bar, Blue Tusk brewery and eatery is another bar that claims to be #1. I didn't believe that claim at first but seeing that they're ranked as one of the 125 places to have a beer before you die from the All About Beer Magazine, it's worth a shot. On tap, they show off a variety of beers from Beak & Skiff 1911 Cider, 3 Floyds Zombie Dust, Maine Lunch, and Great Lakes Edmund Fitzgerald. They also have canned beer like White Claw, draft beers like India Pale Ales, and all the fine wines you could need. If you're hungry, you can get their foods like sliders, quesadillas, soups, salads, and sandwiches with a side of potato salad or dirty potato chips. Here, every hour is happy hour (well, at least until 8 pm) that you can also enjoy with a banquet of up to 50 of your closest friends. I guess they were right about being the #1 place to drink in Syracuse, but I won't get to know until next year. There is a restaurant I can go to and should be given the opportunity.

44. EVERGREEN AND EVERMORE

With an average customer rating of 5 stars on their site (yes, those are real reviews) The Evergreen offers indoor and outdoor eating with many tables available for those who come early enough. On their small plates, they have items like cauliflower wings, poutine, soft pretzel sticks, mac and cheese, and brussel sprouts. They have burgers that come with one side of either beer-battered fries, sriracha fries, rosemary fries, side salads, deviled eggs, and grilled broccolini. There are also sandwiches like grilled chicken, spicy fried chicken, and grilled salmon with the same deal, and house salads, beet, and goat cheese salads, or crispy brussel salads on which you can add avocado, chicken, tofu, or salmon. Now, you can't

Eat Like a Local

have a restaurant in Armory Square without alcohol and from Tuesdays-Sundays, the bar is open to enjoy their drinks like draft beer, bottles, cocktails, sparkling wine, white wine, red wine, whiskey, scotch, tequila, mezcal, vodka, annaro, gin, rum, liquor. Certain specials occur everyday for discounted drinks but they promise to serve the new drinks that they posted and with all the options already available, it seems foolish to pass it up, but if you want something new now, the next place can do it.

45. CAN YA GET SAKANA-YA

If you're looking for Polish food in Armory Square then you're out of luck, but if you need Japanese food, then you have an option. With a lengthy selection of Japanese food and drinks, Sakana-Ya Sushi Bar has the food to fill you up. Appetizers include things such as edamame, summer rolls, gyoza, shrimp dumplings, fried calamari, and crab rangoons. Soups come in the form of miso, gyoza, tom yum, and seafood vegetable while the salads come in the form of house specialties, ika, avocado, spicy Kani, and chef's sashimi. To dig into the more pricey and filling dishes, they got stir fry with almost every meat with vegan options, bento boxes which include shrimp and vegetable tempura, steamed shumai, ika salad, seaweed salad, miso soup, and a side of white rice, nigiri sashimi a la carte with 2-4 pieces, vegetarian rolls, regular rolls, house special rolls, lunch specials, and lunch boxes. Accompanying your delicious dinner, you can have a side of white or brown rice, spicy mayo, Eel sauce, and teriyaki sauce and to drink, you can get sodas, ginger ale, water, or bubble tea. Did someone say another Italian restaurant? Well, I did and so here's another one.

46. TRY NICK'S TOMATO PIE

Okay, last Italian restaurant, I promise, but Nick's Tomato Pie is definitely a restaurant worth mentioning and it's in the area so I'm basically obligated to. Making big promises of big food, Nick's Tomato Pie is another way of saying pizza and they serve up different kinds of Italian food that one would have to smell before it's dealt. Although they don't have a traditional or any website, their Facebook page shows off their pizza instead of telling along with their sense of humor and videos of it. Seeing their pepperoni pizza, surf and turf pizza, chicken pizza, salads, calzones, rolls, wings, and pasta being displayed and made makes it hard to resist as it is so if you're in the area why not give in. They also post any relevant information about when they're opening that day or any holiday specialties they might have on their page or you can ask them any questions through Messenger. They deliver their food nice and fresh but only if you could get the ingredients delivered to your house. Well, you probably didn't say that, but I need to transition to the next place.

47. EATING AT EDEN

Eden is described as an American restaurant open only on Friday, Saturdays, and Sundays for some reason, but it's probably to prepare some of their great food. What makes this restaurant so different is that you can get stuff delivered to you as individual ingredients and food for your own eating pleasure. Their menu is easy to choose from since their locally sourced items can be things like small plates (pan-roasted scallops, burrata, and grilled halloumi), large plates (pan-roasted half chicken, ember roasted hanger steak, and sweet corn ravioli), and grilled peaches as dessert along with their other menu items that come and goes with the seasons. It changes day today, but you can read about it on their blog, but as far as delivery goes, they can give you individual things of dairy products, beef, pork, fruits, vegetables, eggs, honey, maple, bread, salt, spices, beans, vinegar, herbs, and even boxes of either vegetables, protein, or breakfast products. You also donate to the Brady farm as you make your reservation at a restaurant that won the OpenTable Diners' Choice Award and supports local farms and groceries while doing it. But what about Chinese food? I haven't mentioned it yet, but we're getting to it in just a few moments.

48. A CHINA CAFE YOU SAY

At affordable prices, the China Cafe in Syracuse makes it one of the most well known and convenient places to dine in or take out a meal. Their starters seem pretty solid, providing its customers with rolls of different kinds, edamame, scallion pancake, buffalo wings, and a variety of fried foods. Their soups come with a side of crispy noodles and include wonton soup, hot and sour soup, xihu beef soup, and tomato egg drop soup. Their lunches and dinners have tons to offer fried noodles, fried rice, lo mein, mei fun, moo shu, chow mein, egg foo young, and their foods with white rice such as chicken, beef, pork, seafood, sweet and sour, fusion kitchen foods and mixed vegetables. To add on to the list, even more, there is pad thai noodles, ho fun, special Chinese cuisines, dinner combos with roast pork fried rice and an egg roll, and a healthy diet meal you can customize. To drink, they offer up lemonade, tea, soda, coconut, and soybean milk while for dessert they have Chinese cake, sweet soup ball, pineapple chunk, and soybean milk. The only thing this place is missing is a bar, but if only there was yet another bar in the area.

49. WINE AND WHISKEY THAT'S NOT TOO RISKY

Oh, look, another bar in the area. Al's Wine and Whiskey is the premiere bar inside of downtown Syracuse holding the widest amount of wine and whiskey from around the world, or at least that's what they say. The thing that sets this bar aside from the others is that it offers live music, pool, and games you can enjoy while having a drink. So pick your poison, you can have absinthe, arak, & pastis, amaro/bitters, Armagnac, brandy, calvados, cognac, grappa, cordials, gin, rum, cachaca, & pisco, scotch, tequila & mezcal, vodka, or whiskey. Coming from all around the world, those are all of the types of drinks that are offered which can be drunk with your food. As far as the menu goes, there's cheeses, cured meats, salads, and some unauthentic Mexican foods that can come with prosciutto, salsa, guacamole, sour cream, blue cheese, and chips. Like most bars, there are events like Monday night trivia and certain bands playing so

Eat Like a Local

be on the lookout for that too. Why don't bars ever serve desserts? They would be perfect if they had some cookies.

50. COOKIN IN THE COOKIE KITCHEN

Cathy's Cookie Kitchen was founded by Cathy who is a woman passionate about cooking and made her dreams come true through this cookie shop serving her customers the best cookies she can. All of her batches are made with the organic ingredients of butter, eggs, unbleached flour, mix-ins, and of course love. Showing off their collection of cookies, there are so many to choose from such as chocolate, peanut butter, oatmeal raisin, butterscotch, snickers, marshmallow, milky way, caramel pretzel chocolate chip, smores, m&m, cranberry walnut, white chocolate macadamia nut, cupcakes, and so much more. You can even get a batch of dozens worth of cookies if you want to give others a piece of love. If necessary, can even get these cookies vegan or gluten-free and if you're a student at SU, you can join the cookie club to know about their cookie of the month on their website. Syracuse is full of sweet spots, but which ones are the sweetest. I've lived here my whole life, and in my 20 years of living, here are my suggestions.

Eat Like a Local

BONUS TIP 1 THE MALL

I mentioned the mall first for a reason and that reason is that it's basically the heart of Syracuse. Syracuse without Destiny is like a wheel without rubber; sure it still works, but not as well and you just feel something is missing. Hundreds of stores, multiple restaurants, and entertainment from day to night can make people stay at the mall all day which is something most people in Syracuse have done at least once so it is a must for visitors.

BONUS TIP 2 ARMORY SQUARE

Armory Square may not have it all, but it has what the mall doesn't. It doesn't matter if you are a college student hitting the town for the night, a local who needs to blow off steam, or a visitor who wants to see what the fuss is about, Armory Square has a huge chunk of restaurants that was mentioned along with most of the nightlife. Culture, science, fun, and food is anything and everything a tourist could ask for during a vacation, so be there in Armory Square.

BONUS TIP 3 TASTE OF SYRACUSE

There are so many places that I wanted to mention but couldn't due to the fact that there are so many restaurants in Syracuse. Places like Sweet On Chocolate, China Wong, Rio Grande Mexican Restaurant, CopperTop Tavern, and Brooklyn Pickle definitely get honorable mentions, but what if you wanted to try all of these places at once? If you're in Syracuse in the summertime then you can at the Taste of Syracuse. The festival takes place around early June where you can sample dishes from different restaurants for about a single dollar or a little more. Here you can enjoy everything the outdoor festival has to offer including live music, local celebrations, and fundraisers for the local charities as you go tent by tent and vendor by vendor eating at the local restaurant vendors. With all that said, there are so many restaurants to take a bite at and even this only captures a little piece of it. Once you take a dive into Syracuse's mouth first, you might not want to leave this city again.

RESOURCES:

https://www.visitsyracuse.com/

https://www.syracuse.com/food/2017/09/cheap_eats_in_syracuse_25_best_places_to_dine_without_breaking_the_bank.html

https://spoonuniversity.com/place/23-things-eat-syracuse-die

READ OTHER BOOKS BY CZYK PUBLISHING

Greater Than a Tourist- St. Croix US Birgin Islands USA: 50 Travel Tips from a Local by Tracy Birdsall

Greater Than a Tourist- Toulouse France: 50 Travel Tips from a Local by Alix Barnaud

Children's Book: *Charlie the Cavalier Travels the World* by Lisa Rusczyk

Eat Like a Local

Follow *Eat Like a Local* on Amazon.
Join our mailing list for new books
http://bit.ly/EatLikeaLocalbooks

Made in the USA
Las Vegas, NV
08 March 2021